KU-069-432

# Successful
# Intranets
# in a week

## RAY IRVING
## FIONA McWILLIAMS

HAVERING COLLEGE
OF FURTHER & HIGHER EDUCATION

LEARNING RESOURCES
CENTRE

Hodder & Stoughton

A MEMBER OF THE HODDER HEADLINE GROUP

658.05468  A9

107547

# Acknowledgements

The authors and publishers would like to thank the following organisations and people for the use of illustrations and information in this publication: Steve Last of NMGB: Information for Case Study Number 1; Julia Middleton of BT Intranet Services: Information for Case Study Number 2; Jakob Nielsen of Sun Microsystems, Inc: Figure 6; Marni Morowitz of The Mobil Corporation: Information for Case Study Number 3; Sara Wear of Royal & SunAlliance Engineering: Information for Case Study Number 4.

Orders: please contact Bookpoint Ltd, 39 Milton Park, Abingdon, Oxon OX14 4TD. Telephone: (44) 01235 400414, Fax: (44) 01235 400454. Lines are open from 9.00 - 6.00, Monday to Saturday, with a 24 hour message answering service. Email address: orders@bookpoint.co.uk

*British Library Cataloguing in Publication Data*
A catalogue record for this title is available from The British Library

ISBN 0 340 71179 5

First published 1998
Impression number    10  9  8  7  6  5  4  3  2  1
Year                             2004   2003   2002   2001   2000   1999   1998

Copyright © 1998 Ray Irving and Fiona McWilliams

All rights reserved. No part of this publication may be reproduced or transmitted in any form or by any means, electronic or mechanical, including photocopy, recording, or any information storage and retrieval system, without permission in writing from the publisher or under licence from the Copyright Licensing Agency Limited. Further details of such licences (for reprographic reproduction) may be obtained from the Copyright Licensing Agency Limited, of 90 Tottenham Court Road, London W1P 9HE.

Typeset by Multiplex Techniques Ltd, St Mary Cray, Kent.
Printed in Great Britain for Hodder & Stoughton Educational, a division of Hodder Headline Plc, 338 Euston Road, London NW1 3BH by Cox and Wyman, Reading, Berkshire.

**the Institute
of Management**

F O U N D A T I O N

The Institute of Management (IM) exists to promote
the development, exercise and recognition of
professional management. The Institute embraces all
levels of management from student to chief executive
and supports its own Foundation which provides a
unique portfolio of services for all managers, enabling
them to develop skills and achieve management
excellence.

For information on the various levels and benefits of
membership, please contact:

Department HS
Institute of Management
Cottingham Road
Corby
Northants NN17 1TT
Tel: 01536 204222
Fax: 01536 201651

This series is commissioned by the Institute of
Management Foundation.

# C O N T E N T S

# ■ I N T R O D U C T I O N ■

Communication and the sharing of knowledge within organisations have always presented challenges, but getting these two factors right has never before been so important to an organisation's success. One of the most recent developments to improve organisational information flow has been the combination of computer networking and Internet technology, allowing employees to communicate and share information more freely.

This combination of computer network, Internet software and easily accessible corporate information is known as an *Intranet*. Intranets have been heralded as the most important corporate technological application ever to emerge, and one which organisations in the future will base their whole structures around. Millions of employees all around the world will eventually come to rely on Intranets to carry out their work, and managers will need to play an important role in ensuring that information required for organisational success is available on their Intranet, and that it is used to its best effect.

In *Successful Intranets in a Week* we will define what an Intranet is, explain the hardware and software needed to utilise one and put forward a planning process for building an Intranet. We will also examine what an Intranet can do and the associated management and legal issues.

# What is an Intranet?

Although often viewed with scepticism, new developments in information technology are beginning to impact on the way business is carried out. The fax machine is now viewed as an essential tool of business, and video-conferencing and **e-mail** are fast following in its footsteps. These have made a considerable impact on internal corporate communications, but a more recent development, the Intranet, is being touted as the most dramatic change which corporate communication has undergone.

Today, we will take a broad, introductory look at Intranets. We shall look at how they have developed and what they can do, before setting one up over the week.

We're not going to dwell on the technological aspects just yet, but we will begin to introduce some of the key terms that will be used throughout the week. If you need a refresher for any of the terms, there is a glossary at the end of the book. By the end of today, we will have clarified:

- What is the Internet?
- How does the Internet work, and what can we do on it?
- Why is the Internet important?
- What is an Intranet?
- What can we do with an Intranet?
- What are the business benefits offered by Intranets?
- What advantages do Intranets have over the Internet?
- Are there any drawbacks to setting up an Intranet?
- What type of organisation can use an Intranet?

# What is the Internet?

In order to be able to understand the concept of Intranets, we need to examine how they developed. This involves looking at the *Internet*, which is where the enabling technology for Intranets was developed.

The Internet is a global network of networks linked together into a super-network. It comprises millions of computers around the world, and has many millions of users. Nobody 'owns' the Internet, it is simply there, and nobody has ever been able to compile accurate statistics as to its size because it is growing all the time.

# How does the Internet work?

In order to connect to the Internet, most individuals use a *personal computer (PC)* with a **modem** to connect through an **Internet Service Provider (ISP)** such as Pipex or Demon. (Some people or organisations have a permanent connection to the Internet where an individual modem is not required.) The diagram overleaf illustrates the topology of the Internet.

Here, we have only shown five **servers** (computers which contain the information available over the Internet), but when you consider that there are many hundreds of thousands of these world-wide, then you will begin to get some idea of the size of the Internet. These servers are situated at universities, schools, businesses, government departments, almost anywhere you can think of, throughout the world. In turn, there can be far more than the two computers attached to each of these servers. Millions of individuals world-wide subscribe to ISPs. Once connected, you have access to information stored anywhere on the Internet, and can communicate with all of the attached computers.

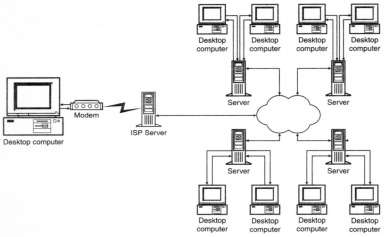

**Figure 1** *The topology of the Internet*

## What can we do on the Internet?

There are three main things you can do when you have connected to the Internet, all of which enable communication. You can transfer data, research information and take part in discussions. These utilise three important Internet tools:

*E-mail*
**E-mail (electronic mail)** is a medium of interpersonal communication. Millions of people who use the Internet have their own specific e-mail address. It has the immediacy of a telephone call, without the all-too-common problem of failing to find someone at their desk, or their line engaged.

*World Wide Web*

The **World Wide Web (WWW)** is a collection of graphical *pages* of information. These pages are linked via a technology called **HyperText** which enables you (through links built into the page by the author) to move from one point on a page to related information on the same page, site or elsewhere on the Internet. Placing information on the WWW is not restricted to large organisations or to those with computer expertise. The information in these pages varies widely, from marketing details (a description of a product), or the full text of a report, to the latest news on a football team. Increasingly, organisations are placing pictures and text about their products on a WWW page and then allowing users to order them by sending their credit-card details over the Internet.

Access to the WWW is available to anyone with an Internet connection who also has a *Web browser*: a piece of software which provides a graphical interface to the information held.

All pages on the WWW have a unique address: a **Uniform Resource Locator (URL)**. Once this is typed into a browser, you will be taken to the selected page. There are numerous *search engines* which can also be used to find areas of interest on the WWW, but they are not particularly intelligent; searches can yield thousands of sites, some more relevant than others.

Here are some examples of organisations that have Web sites on the Internet. Remember that sites can appear overnight:

- http://www.inst-mgt.org.uk – the Institute of Management
- http://www.microsoft.com – web site for the software giant

- http://www.ft.com – the *Financial Times* newspaper
- http://www.yahoo.com – an Internet search engine
- http://www.yell.co.uk – UK Yellow Pages

*Newsgroups and discussion lists*

**Newsgroups** and **discussion lists** are synonymous terms for a medium through which people with Internet access can swap news and gossip, discuss new developments in their field, ask each other questions and send and receive information and advice.

Here are two examples of newsgroups and discussion lists that you can find on the Internet:

- uk.telecom – discussion on BT and the provision of telecommunication services in the UK
- comp.lang.c++ – a group dedicated to the use of the C++ programming language

## Why is the Internet important?

The massive growth in popularity of the Internet over the last five years has for the most part been because of the development of the graphical interface of the WWW. The possibilities offered by the Internet include:

- Instant availability of massive amounts of information, mostly free of charge
- Internet access (and coverage) world-wide
- Cheap communications – when you consider that you can contact any country for just the price of a local call
- Up-to-the-minute information which can be made available world-wide instantly

There are, however, some downsides to the Internet.

- It can be very slow – downloading files or viewing Web pages at peak times (when a lot of people are connected) can be slow (afternoons are particularly bad as people in both Europe and America are accessing the Internet at the same time)
- The lack of a control structure means that anyone can put anything they want on the Internet
- It can be quite hard to find specific information due to the huge quantities available

## What is an Intranet?

An Intranet is a private, corporate network that uses Internet products and technologies. Access to an Intranet is controlled by the organisation which established it, and is often restricted just to employees. Occasionally, however, suppliers or customers can also be given access to parts of it. (This latter type of Intranet is known as an *Extranet*.)

Just as we can see text and graphics pages on the World
Wide Web, or download a file from another computer, or
send someone an e-mail message on the Internet, we can do
the same within our own organisation using the same tools
and techniques.

Intranets work on exactly the same principle as the
Internet. A server holds the information, and computers
attached to it can access some or all of that information.
Take a look at the diagram of a simple Intranet.

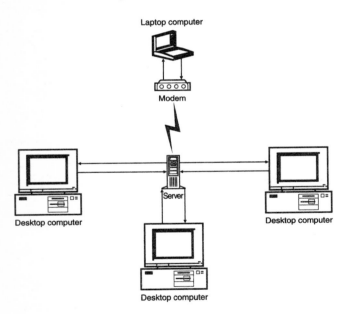

**Figure 2** *A Local Area Network for the Intranet*

In this case we only have three desktop computers attached
to the server and one laptop computer that can access the
Intranet by *dialling-in* using a modem. Again, there could

be thousands of computers connected to the server; it all depends on how many computers you have that you wish to connect. These single-site networks are called **Local Area Networks (LANs)**.

Alternatively, if you have a number of sites, nationally or globally, you can connect them all up – see the diagram.

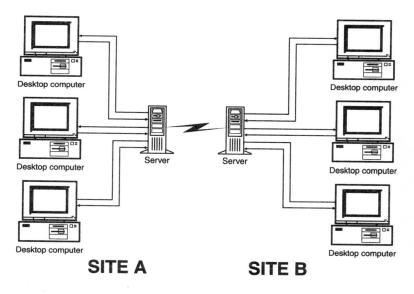

**SITE A**          **SITE B**

**Figure 3**   *A Wide Area Network for the Intranet*

These are called **Wide Area Networks (WANs)**. Connections between these sites are usually by means of a **leased line**, although these can also be made via the Internet (this has security implications which we will consider on Tuesday).

Information on Site A's server can be accessed by computers at Site B in one of two ways: either by requesting information to be downloaded directly to the computer from Site A (which can be time consuming) or by duplicating all the information onto a server at Site B (this is known as a **mirror site**). This is obviously quicker than the first option, but requires careful management to ensure the currency of information on the mirror server.

## What can we do with an Intranet?

The options offered by an Intranet are extensive and are only really limited by the requirements of the organisation. To begin to generate ideas of the possibilities available, make a list of the type of information you could put on a server to which all staff have access.

Maybe these scenarios will help:

- Instead of sending a paper copy of a memo, minutes of a meeting, or newsletters to every employee in your organisation, all these could be placed on a server, and everyone could then access the information from their desktop computer.
- You're going to a meeting and there will be someone there from another department whom you have spoken to many times on the telephone but have never met. Why not first view their photograph on the list of personnel on the Intranet Web site?
- Have you ever worked from home, or been at a customer's office, and needed to search through your company's product catalogue and find the most up-to-date prices? And then needed to know if there were any particular products in stock? Why not connect to the company's Intranet with your laptop computer and modem?

These scenarios only just begin to demonstrate the possible applications of an Intranet.

Some typical such applications include:

- Staff training
- Internal databases
- Newsletters
- Job vacancies
- Telephone lists
- Sharing of management information
- Staff handbooks

On Wednesday we'll look more closely at the internal applications for an Intranet. Ways in which you can open up your Intranet to improve relations and information flows with your suppliers and customers through an Extranet are examined on Thursday.

## What are the business benefits of Intranets?

Intranets offer some clear business benefits. They are a technology which enables better communication. Better communication has a direct impact on the quality of customer service, which is one of the most important competitive advantages an organisation can achieve. Intranets can provide:

- Faster and easier access to more up-to-date company information
- Faster and better communication among employees
- Instant access to product and service information
- Reduced paper distribution via the replacement of printed material with electronic publications
- Improved collaboration on projects
- Conduits to facilitate flexible working; employees can access the same information at any site or even from their own home

## What advantages does an Intranet have over the Internet?

An Intranet offers all the advantages of the Internet, but because it is your own network – and control can therefore be exercised over its content and access to it – it offers additional benefits. Intranets:

- Enable the publication of company confidential material
- Are more manageable and more controllable for the organisation. *We* decide what information is included on our Intranet and who has access to it

- Are faster than the Internet – they do not have to rely on phone lines, and there are fewer users, reducing the amount of traffic
- Limit the amount of information to be searched – a search will be more specific and will result in a higher percentage of useful *hits*

## Are there any drawbacks to setting up an Intranet?

The pros of setting up an Intranet seem pretty convincing, but we should consider the following points before embarking on implementation:

- Intranets require an investment in resources, usually more in staff time than in capital expenditure. An Intranet is not a project which can be absorbed into daily working time. For an Intranet to be kept up-to-date, continuous effort is required: if it is *not* kept up-to-date, then it will become moribund and gradually less useful for day-to-day work. If your organisation is only prepared to put in a minimum amount of staff time, then you should think again about whether or not to implement an Intranet.

- Technology is continually changing. New applications for the Intranet become available, some free and others requiring payment. To have an efficient Intranet, you need to keep up with, and utilise, these developments.

## What type of organisation can benefit from an Intranet?

Communication and knowledge are essential to all types of organisation; private or public sector, manufacturing or service companies, and large, medium and small alike. Here are some examples of companies that have implemented Intranets:

- The Institute of Management
- Glaxo-Wellcome
- Levi Strauss
- Ford Motor Company
- Booz Allen & Hamilton
- Albion Oil
- Cap Gemini

# Case Study No. 1 – Nissan Online

Nissan Motor (GB) – NMGB – is the marketing and distribution arm of Nissan in the UK, selling about 100,000 cars a year. It supports a distributed network of 270 franchised (but independent) dealerships.

NMGB manages a network of about 1,200 workstations over an **Integrated Services Digital Network (ISDN)** line. The network was set up some time ago using TCP/IP as the protocol. As technology developed, it was decided to take full advantage of Internet technology and implement an Intranet which, with links to the dealers, would become an Extranet. This was Nissan Online.

Nissan Online was launched in May 1997, and is still evolving. NMGB uses the Extranet as the primary method of delivering new applications to its dealers, as well as significantly improving ease of access to the information available – and indeed of increasing the amount and scope of that information. Recently, the mobile workforce has been added to the network: business reports can now be delivered without having to support applications on individual laptops.

NMGB's Extranet makes use of a separate interface for each set of users:

- Head office staff have an interface which reflects the business departments and internal structure
- Remote users have access to both the Intranet and the Extranet, plus an interface which utilises dynamic links and is entirely driven by database access
- Dealers use a set of pages which represent the different activities in a dealer showroom

The contents of the dealer Web include:

- *Parts* – which is used to publicise campaigns and pricing information
- *Sales* – which gives vehicle availability, comparative data

between models and manufacturers, and fleet information

- *Marketing* – all the information to support marketing initiatives is being made available electronically
- *Service* – all service and technical bulletins have been digitised and are made available through queries to a central database
- *Training* – information on the range of training courses provided is published here. A range of tests and quizzes is also run, with progress and results recorded centrally
- *In the News* – press releases, interesting data and wider interests (such as the British Touring Car Championship) receive full coverage so that dealers are aware of Nissan's presence in the market
- *Infinet* – this enables a dealer to find information on how the NMGB dealer systems work, and to order new machines
- *Dealer Principal* – this comprises all information a dealer principal needs to run their business better
- *Nissan Finance* – the new finance company has written its point-of-sale application as an Intranet which is 'fed' onto the Extranet. Information on the services provided by this company is also available

The contents of the Extranet are indexed via Microsoft Index, which enables a fast search facility for all material published.

*Information provided by Mr Steve Last of NMGB*

## Summary

To sum up what we have discussed today:

- Communication is integral to all aspects of work
- The Internet is a sprawling, global network of computers that allows us to communicate and share information with other users

- There are many problems with the Internet, chiefly its lack of structure and slowness, but it has many benefits, especially in that it is easy to use
- An Intranet is a private, organisational network that uses the same hardware and software as the Internet, but is more controllable and is much faster
- All organisations can use an Intranet to harness, develop and communicate their knowledge and information resources

Tomorrow we will begin to plan our Intranet.

# Getting started

Today we will look at the initial stages of setting up
an Intranet.

Setting up an Intranet is like implementing any other
information system. The technological aspects are
obviously important, but the rules of project management
must also be followed if the Intranet is to succeed.

There are six stages critical to the setting-up and running of
an Intranet. These are demonstrated in the chart shown.
This process is commonly referred to as the *project life cycle*.

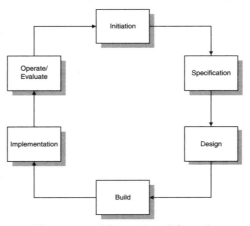

**Figure 4**   *The project life cycle*

1  *Initiation.* This is where we: gain the backing of
   senior management; appoint a project co-ordinator;
   bring together a project team; and set objectives for
   our Intranet.
2  *Specification.* By looking into the background of
   Intranets, viewing some Intranets already in

operation, and analysing our communication needs, we can draw up the specifications for our organisation's own tailor-made Intranet.

We will concentrate on these first two stages today.

3 *Design.* From our specification – the 'what we want our Intranet to do' stage – we can draw up a detailed plan, including the configuration of hardware and software needed. On Tuesday we will look at the hardware and software issues.

4 *Build.* We now put the Intranet together. Our hardware and software is set up, and the 'information content' for our Intranet is prepared. We'll look at the design of content and the building stages in more detail on Wednesday, and on Thursday we will show how the Intranet can be expanded outside the organisation.

5 *Implementation.* Once everything is in place, we can put our Intranet into operation and let staff, customers and suppliers 'loose' on it. This means we need to educate the users of the Intranet, not only on finding information but also on creating it. This is considered on Friday.

6 Operate/Evaluate. Continually appraising and reviewing the Intranet is essential. We need to be aware of who is and who isn't using the Intranet, and to make modifications where necessary. Constant promotion and development of the Intranet is also required. Saturday considers the operational and evaluation stages.

This systematic approach to building and running the Intranet allows for full control of the project, with defined responsibilities and objectives that are agreed upon by all parties.

## Initiating the Intranet project

To establish and run an Intranet, we need to:

- Obtain senior management commitment
- Appoint a project manager
- Bring together an Intranet team
- Give the Intranet a name
- Gather background information
- Ascertain what resources are available
- Set objectives for the Intranet
- Identify our requirements
- Put together an Intranet implementation plan

Let's look at these points in more detail.

*Obtain senior management commitment*
To work successfully, an Intranet requires visible commitment from the top levels of management within the organisation. This is because the project needs money and resources from across the organisation (and only senior managers are in a position to obtain across-the-board resources). Additionally, Intranets are about knowledge, and they can therefore appear to threaten the power base of many individuals. Senior management commitment ensures that everyone recognises that the Intranet is a key project and will provide the project team with sufficient 'clout' to get things done.

*Appoint a project manager*

The project manager has overall responsibility for the Intranet's introduction and maintenance. Ideally, they should be someone already well known and respected within the organisation; someone with an overall understanding of the organisation's activities, the underlying business case for the Intranet and at least a basic knowledge of IT.

The key skills the project manager must have include an ability to:

- Motivate
- Delegate
- Communicate
- Lead
- Co-ordinate

If such a person is not readily available, you may wish to buy in this expertise.

*Bring together an Intranet team*

The most important appointee to the project team will be the person who will eventually become a **webmaster**.

A webmaster is usually a person who combines technical knowledge of Intranets (or the Internet) with document-editing and management skills. The webmaster is responsible for the overall management and maintenance of the site.

In addition to the project manager and webmaster, the other team members should comprise a mix of staff from the organisation. This is because one of the main reasons why many computer systems do not live up to expectations is that they have been designed and implemented by those people who will not be using them! If staff are unable to see a use for the Intranet, or don't like it, they will not use it and it will fail. When putting together an Intranet project team, it is therefore essential to include representatives of staff from all levels and in all areas.

A good mix of project team staff would include:

- Key decision-makers from management and finance
- A webmaster
- Existing IT staff
- One member from each function – personnel, research and development etc.
- An individual who is unlikely to be responsible for any content, but will be an *end-user* once the Intranet is live

To be manageable, a project team should ideally not consist of more than six individuals who can meet regularly.

Remember as well that if you are going to extend your Intranet to customers and suppliers, they need to be on-board and involved from the start (this is a key factor in the planning stage).

By the end of this stage, we can see a hierarchy developing for our Intranet's implementation – see the diagram opposite.

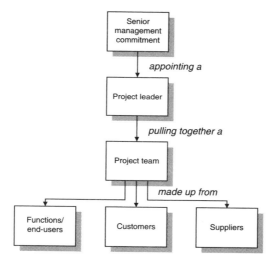

**Figure 5** *Hierarchy of Intranet development*

*Give the Intranet a name*

Now the project team has been established, the time has come to give the proposed Intranet a name (and therefore an identity). Giving it an identity helps people to realise that the Intranet *is* going to happen, and it means that you can begin to promote it. The design of the Intranet logo can be built around this, and if paper (hard-copy) reports are to be sent out on the Intranet's progress, they can incorporate this as well.

The name should be short and simple – at the most, three words long.

Here are three examples of Intranets:

- Sun Microcomputers – 'SunWeb'
- British Broadcasting Corporation (BBC) – 'Gateway'
- Booz Allen & Hamilton – 'Knowledge On Line' (KOL)

*Gather background information*

Another early step for members of the project management team is a site visit to an organisation which already uses an Intranet. The computer press and the Internet itself will provide possible contacts. Be aware of:

- The applications used – is anything especially innovative being used?
- The hardware and software required – how does this compare to your existing resources?
- The composition of the management and maintenance team – how does the partnership work on a day-to-day basis?
- The content providers and creators – where does responsibility lie? Do all parts of the organisation contribute?

Get a general feel for the Intranet and ask what advantages or benefits it can bring the organisation, in terms not only of cost-savings but also of improved communication and information flow (which are often hard to quantify). If you get the chance, talk to those people who are actually using it to ascertain their views. Organisations may be cautious about telling you too much, though, as Intranets are seen very clearly as a source of competitive advantage, and telling others can diminish this!

After such a visit, the Intranet team will be brimming with ideas and enthusiasm to get on with setting up their own Intranet. At this stage you may be able to form closer partnership links with another organisation to share ideas on Intranets.

*Ascertain what resources are available*

While you can now see what an Intranet can do, and are keen to get started, you must first establish what resources are available to you. This will highlight possibilities as well as limitations and help you gain a realistic picture. These resources fall into three categories:

- Computers
- People
- Money/budget

*Computers*: Tomorrow we'll take a look in detail at the hardware and software needed to build the Intranet, but first it is important that we check and acknowledge what we already have in place. Depending on the organisation, there may be an existing network of computers or there may be an unco-ordinated scattering of PCs on a number of desks. The IT member of the Intranet project team will be able to put some figures together to give an idea of how much it will cost to upgrade existing resources so as to network the whole organisation.

*People*: Here, we need first to establish how many employees we envisage using the Intranet, and then to assess what skills are available in each department and function. When the Intranet is in operation, staff will need to be trained so that they have the skills to put together their own information content. Remember that one of the most important facets of an Intranet is that the information held on it is up-to-date. Staff time *must* be available throughout the organisation to allow this to happen.

*Budget*: For most organisations, this will be the most critical point. The financial resources made available for the project will determine what we can achieve with our Intranet. Find out if the capital to fund it can be made available. Will the IT department be expected to fund it from its current budget, or will all departments be expected to contribute? Marked savings usually occur when an Intranet is implemented, but these will obviously only materialise after the event and are not always spread equally throughout the organisation (reprographic departments will notice a drop in the amount of paper used, but other departments will not automatically see the cost savings; productivity may increase – but the improvement may be hard to ascribe to the Intranet). The project team will need to be able to *sell* the business benefits of the Intranet in order to secure funding from all departments.

What are the typical items of expenditure?

- Computer hardware
- Computer software
- Consultancy fees

- Extra personnel
- Training

Remember that costs will continue as the project evolves.

*Set objectives for the Intranet*
When the budget is set, it will then be possible to set realistic objectives. An all-singing, all-dancing Intranet cannot be implemented on a budget of £2,000, so be realistic! In fact, if money seems hard to obtain, you need to question the commitment of the senior managers who inaugurated the project.

By setting objectives, we are providing, among other things, a direction for our Intranet project. Typical objectives may include:

- Improving communication and information flow amongst employees, suppliers and customers

- Improving customer service
- Allowing new ways of working, including teleworking and 'hot-desking'
- Facilitating cross-functional teams and projects

Keep your objectives in mind at all times throughout the Intranet project.

We must define who is going to be affected by the introduction of our Intranet. One of the major benefits of Intranets is that they are *scaleable*. That is, they can be implemented piece-by-piece; so personnel information and company news could be placed on the Intranet first, then product information, followed by sales information.

Implementing the Intranet in stages is the safest route to follow and means that a pilot version can be assessed before the project is implemented fully. Processes and procedures can be worked out and fine-tuned and can then be applied to the other areas. Many computer experts agree that the reason IT projects fail is that they are implemented in a 'big bang'. Lessons can be learned from the 'pilot' project that will help when the Intranet expands to take on board more applications.

*Identify our requirements*
You may have a large number of ideas for Intranet applications, but like any other computing solution, an Intranet needs a firm organisation-wide communications structure to support it. Establish what the current communications infrastructure of your organisation is through a communications audit, which maps the flow of information in your organisation.

This audit will identify who needs what information and who is sharing it. Personnel information, like a staff handbook or telephone directory, will need to be made available to all employees. Other information, like sales figures, may only need to be seen by finance, sales and marketing. Stock figures could be essential to suppliers, customers or on the shop floor.

Each member of the Intranet team should answer the following questions through a survey of their department, based on real needs – not on the 'nice to have' criterion:

- Take a look at your desk and in-tray. Which bits of paper do you see (e.g. newsletters or memos)? Who publishes them? What else do they publish?
- What information do you need to do your job? Where do you get it from, and how long does it take for you to get it?
- What information do you provide for others (e.g. monthly reports)?

The experiences of the Intranet team will enable a list of the critical information 'sets' for the organisation to be produced, including:

- Policies and procedures
- Departmental and personal strengths
- Ongoing projects and initiatives

*Put together an Intranet implementation plan*
Once the above stages have been worked through, we can put together an Intranet implementation plan. This will detail the applications we are going to use the Intranet for, the scope of the Intranet, and a timetable for action. Each Intranet plan will be unique, depending on the resources available and the nature of the organisation. An example plan would look something like this:

### *IntraBloggs Intranet Implementation Plan*

**Stage 1:**

- Application – personnel information (e.g. staff handbook, job vacancies)
- Scope – all sales staff (70 employees) at Bridgeville
- Deadline – December 1998

**Stage 2:**

- Expansion of Stage 1 to include all staff at Bridgeville site
- Deadline – February 1999

**Further developments:**

- Application – marketing and sales information (e.g. advertisements, catalogues)
- Scope – all sales staff (70 employees) at Bridgeville
- Deadline – April 1999

Remember, this plan will only really serve as a guideline. As experience is gained of managing and developing an Intranet, the rate of implementation will increase or problems may slow the implementation calendar. You must be prepared, therefore, to amend the plan to produce a realistic picture. Notice how the staged implementation should allow time for any problems to be solved.

## Summary

By the end of today we are now in a position where:

- We have someone in charge of the project
- The main people involved in the introduction of the Intranet are part of a team
- A name has been given to the Intranet
- We have a list of objectives
- Those functions and areas that will be affected by the Intranet have been identified
- The resources that are currently available have been calculated
- A plan and timetable have been put together for the Intranet's implementation

Tomorrow we will look at the hardware and software that will enable us to put our plans into action.

# What hardware and software are needed?

Having planned out an Intranet, today we will look in detail at the hardware and software needed to run it.

A standard configuration for an Intranet consists of a computer network and WWW server software plus a **client browser** which enables users to view the information held. In setting up an Intranet, the following components must be considered:

- Computer network
- WWW server software
- WWW client browser software
- Web publishing tools
- Security issues
- Usage tracking tools
- Search engine
- Discussion-group server software

It is possible to buy a complete Intranet *solution* which contains these items (apart from the hardware that makes up the network) and provides security solutions, but as most organisations already have some or all of the above and wish to make use of them, many opt for a 'do-it-yourself' approach.

When making decisions about the type of system you intend to develop, you need to ask yourself:

- What information do we intend to hold?
- How easy will the system be to set up?
- Can the system be integrated into existing technical resources and supported by current staff?
- How extensive is the range of tools we already have which can be used to develop our Intranet?
- What tools do we need to develop our Intranet?
- Is the system able to support the intended number of users?

As we take a closer look at the various components of an Intranet, bear these questions in mind.

## The computer network

The *computer network* forms the backbone of an Intranet. A computer network *must* consist of certain (essential) components:

- A group of computers
- Network operating software
- Cabling to link the computers together
- A network adapter for each computer you wish to link

Beyond these, much depends on the type of network you require. Many organisations already have a computer network, and often this will be suitable for running the corporate Intranet. If not, setting up a network is not as complicated as it sounds.

First, what is a computer network? A network links some or all of the computers within an organisation together so that they may share resources or information. This is done via information passing around the network from one computer to the next, or to the central computer. To avoid messages bumping into each other, standard *protocols* have been developed – the most widely used of which is TCP/IP.

There are a variety of network types available, and as the network is so integral to the Intranet, we'll look at the options for these first. Three main avenues exist for Intranet networks:

- Peer to peer – this is the simplest and cheapest type of network
- Web server – the standard form of Intranet
- Web server with dynamic information links – the fusion of Web server and corporate information systems

Apart from differences in price, each of these forms of network has different facilities and advantages and disadvantages over the others. The type of organisation (and the Intranet you will build) will have some bearing on which of the networks is most appropriate.

*Peer-to-peer networking*
To operate over a peer-to-peer network, an Intranet would be made up of individual users publishing their own Web pages for use by the group.

*Web-server networking*
This form of Intranet allows for centralised document provision. All pages are held in a central computer and can be accessed by anyone on the computer network. It can be likened to a library, where a store of documents is held in one place with a librarian (or in the case of an Intranet a *webmaster*) responsible for their management.

*Web-server networking with dynamic links*
This is a step up from a Web-server Intranet. The addition of dynamic links here means that the Intranet can act as a front-end to software packages. This provides access through a common interface (the **browser**) to individual packages with which individuals need not be familiar.

Dynamic links allow the presentation of organisational software packages and data through a Web interface. In other words, client browsers are given access to information held not directly on the Intranet but in other sources on the server. These might include:

- Accounts information
- SQL databases
- Spreadsheet packages

Although normal Web-server packages can be used for this type of networking, complex programming is required to ensure they work properly. Dedicated software packages such as Lotus Domino (www.lotus.com) are a simpler option.

## The software required

Now that we've discussed the hardware and operating systems required for setting up a network, we can begin to look at the software we will need, including:

- Browsers
- Web publishing tools
- Security systems
- Usage tracking tools
- Search engines
- Mail/discussion-group software

*Browsers*

As we saw on Sunday, the content of an Intranet is made up of *pages* of material. These pages are viewed through a piece of software which acts as a *front-end* to them. The generic name for these front-ends is *browser*. A wide range of browsers exists, but the functions offered by each are remarkably similar to those of the others.

Netscape Navigator and Microsoft Internet Explorer are the two most widely known. The early versions of Netscape were given away free, and it has consequently developed a loyal following despite it now being charged for. Microsoft Internet Explorer (IE) came on to the market considerably later, but due to Microsoft's world-wide spread (and the fact that IE is now an integral part of Windows) it has made up a lot of ground.

A copy of whichever browser you choose must be installed on each computer that you wish to have access to your Intranet. Although standards ratified by the World Wide Web Consortium (W3C) exist, the major suppliers of browsers have been trying to add extra functionality to their software. This has led to some slight inconsistencies in the way information is displayed in each browser. Consequently, for simplicity's sake, only one variety of browser should be used throughout the organisation. This will also help in the future management of the Intranet as you will need to ensure that you have the most up-to-date version of only one type of browser.

*Web publishing tools*
Internet and Intranet Web pages are written in an easy-to-use language known as **HTML** (or **HyperText Markup Language**). HTML editors are widely available over the Internet, and names include Hot Metal and Front Page. In the past it was essential to know how to use HTML in order to set up Web pages. It is still advantageous if HTML expertise is available to you, but many word-processing packages now have an in-built facility for creating and editing HTML documents, relieving you of much of the work.

*Security issues*

Because Intranets are a closed, internal network, you may wonder why security is important – after all, only your employees will be able to gain access to the information. Also, security mechanisms will add to the overall complexity of your Intranet and will make little visible difference to the end-users. However, security for your Intranet is an imperative.

By the very nature of the information they hold, Intranets are key targets for computer hackers or competitors – where else could they find in one place details of personnel, product development and financial information? Disenchanted employees may also see opportunities for sabotage. Intranet security, then, is of the highest importance, and its requirements must be recognised from the first discussions.

A range of techniques or technologies for security exists:

- *Password protection.* Password protection is a cheap and fairly standard method to protect any computer system from unauthorised access. Password protection can also be used to restrict access to some parts of the site for certain people – not everyone needs access to accounts information, for example. However, password protection is fairly limited in what it can do.
- *Firewalls.* Firewalls form a barrier between the files/documents and illegal users (or legal users wishing to carry out unauthorised activity), and are a mechanism which ensures that all requests come through permitted pathways. They can also limit access to information to specific machines (for example, accounts pages can be accessed

only by computers within the accounts department). The main drawback to firewalls is that they are complicated to set up.

- *Detection of intruders.* Even with security systems in place, you need some form of tracking software to establish whether anyone is getting through your security. An audit tool which measures the use of your Intranet may well help you spot a suspicious amount of activity over the network – although as you expect use to be made of the Intranet, this may be difficult to spot.

- *Encryption.* Encryption has only recently begun to be considered viable for commercial use – and even then it is mostly used just to hide messages being transmitted, not to code stored files. New software developments are, however, making this a more feasible option.

Whichever option (or options) you choose, it is important that it be employed organisation-wide.

Additionally, there is the important human element to security. User-education is essential. Security systems are designed to be effective, but if users are unaware of why security measures exist, and that the information contained within the Intranet is confidential, there is always the danger of an unintentional security breach. This risk to security is higher on Intranets than on other forms of corporate information-technology usage, as many people are now aware of the fact that most information on the Internet is freely available and may not draw a distinction between the Internet and their Intranet.

## Usage tracking tools

The content of an Intranet is like any other form of
publication: it is essential to receive feedback on it and
to know what are the most and least widely used parts.
On an Intranet it is possible to track this sort of information
by automatically recording the number of visits each page
receives through usage tracking software.

A wide range of tools exists to enable this analysis. Most
operate via log files that record such information as the
date and time of the connection, the pages requested and
where the request came from. This means that you could
find that the latest press release on the Intranet had been
looked at 350 times. The more sophisticated the package
used, the more control the webmaster will have over the
type of report created – information may be produced
daily or monthly, and some even allow the creation of
*instant* figures.

## Search engines

Search engines allow visitors to find information held on
your Intranet. They operate in the same way as those on
the Internet (such as Yahoo! or Excite). Most search engines
prepare their indices automatically, from the text within
the pages.

## Discussion-group software

We discussed on Sunday the capabilities of discussion
groups. Groups can be set up on an Intranet in exactly the
same way as those on the Internet – Microsoft Exchange or
Lotus Notes are examples of the type of package which can
host them.

## Summary

Today we have examined the hardware and software which make up an Intranet. There are some useful sites on the Internet where you can obtain up-to-date information on tools and developments, including:

- www.brint.com – a site with details on a huge range of Intranet-related subjects
- www.microsoft.com – for information on Microsoft Internet Explorer
- www.netscape.com – for information on Netscape Navigator
- www.lotus.com – for information on Lotus Domino

# Internal applications of Intranets

Today we will look at the 'Design' and 'Build' stages of our Intranet project cycle. In doing so we will examine:

- Intranet applications
- Intranet design
- Content design
- Putting it all together – assigning responsibility

## Intranet applications

Although there are some things which are equally important to all organisations (such as staff handbooks and telephone directories), the type of information you put on your Intranet is very much dependent on your organisation. The information and communication audit we discussed on Monday will have provided you with many ideas for applications.

The content of an Intranet can be divided into two types: flat content and interactive content.

*Flat content*
A list (to help you begin to think about your existing information) of some of the internal Intranet applications in use in some organisations follows. The type of content in this list is fairly static – consequently, it is known as *flat* content. Tick the boxes alongside as you identify which would be applicable to your organisation and whether you could do away with paper versions altogether. Bear in mind that the information in each application will be up-to-date and accessible to employees wherever they are.

|  | Applicable | Replace paper |
|---|:---:|:---:|
| Organisation mission and value statements | ❑ | ❑ |
| Forthcoming events and conferences | ❑ | ❑ |
| Company magazines | ❑ | ❑ |
| Minutes of important meetings | ❑ | ❑ |
| Annual report | ❑ | ❑ |
| Financial news and sales figures | ❑ | ❑ |
| New contracts awarded/orders won | ❑ | ❑ |
| Organisation chart | ❑ | ❑ |
| Product and service guides | ❑ | ❑ |
| New employee information | ❑ | ❑ |
| Travel aids (maps, best routes etc.) | ❑ | ❑ |
| Frequently Asked Questions (FAQs) | ❑ | ❑ |
| Organisational facilities (i.e. canteen, sports) | ❑ | ❑ |
| Staff benefits | ❑ | ❑ |
| Work scheduling | ❑ | ❑ |
| Software downloads (including upgrades and patches/bug fixes) | ❑ | ❑ |
| Catalogues and price lists | ❑ | ❑ |
| Press releases | ❑ | ❑ |
| Employee diaries | ❑ | ❑ |
| Management reports | ❑ | ❑ |
| Stock/inventory levels | ❑ | ❑ |
| ISO 9000 documentation/ quality manuals | ❑ | ❑ |
| Staff training (can use multimedia – audio and video) | ❑ | ❑ |
| Design specifications/diagrams | ❑ | ❑ |

Employee 'classifieds' ❑ ❑
New-product information ❑ ❑
Newsletters ❑ ❑
Job descriptions ❑ ❑
Project tracking ❑ ❑
Instruction manuals ❑ ❑
Software and hardware user guides ❑ ❑
Customers', suppliers' and dealers' details ❑ ❑
Job vacancies ❑ ❑
Telephone lists and 'potted biographies' ❑ ❑
Staff handbooks ❑ ❑
'Guided tours' of the organisation ❑ ❑
  and the Intranet

*Interactive content*

**Interactive** content changes frequently, and can be dynamic. It can produce different responses to individual requirements, and it enables the easy manipulation of data. Interactive content often works in the following way:

Your organisation may wish to share information on customers between the sales team, marketing department and customer support. As soon as the sales team inputs the details of a customer through a form on the Intranet, the marketing department will have immediate access to the information, and the support department will know exactly what the customer bought, when and where, at the same time.

FLAT CONTENT         INTERACTIVE CONTENT

As a general rule, interactive applications require the type of networks discussed yesterday which enable dynamic links. Hosting your internal databases on the Intranet may require new software and even programming skills to develop HTML screens to enable the information to be viewed over the Intranet. Other interactive applications, like video-conferencing, require new software and capable hardware on the user's and provider's sides.

Here are a few examples of interactive content applications:

- Registration facilities for internal training courses
- Suggestion boxes
- Skills databases
- Real-time sales figures
- Online 'conferencing' facilities
- Internal databases (e.g. research and library databases)

The scaleable nature of Intranets can be put to good use when the two types of content are considered. First, the straightforward 'flat' content can be implemented, and then the development can be rolled forward to encompass interactive content.

Don't worry if your Intranet seems small in scope at first. As the benefits of an Intranet become more obvious to employees, wider recognition will mean you will be inundated with ideas for new applications and content.

## Case Study No. 2 – BT's Intranet

Following a trial of a small departmental Intranet, BT decided in January 1995 that the path to *information sanity* lay in implementing its own corporate Intranet for its 65,000 staff. Previously, as BT's Electronic Communications Manager explains, 'We had a *push-me* system in place that just pushed information out. We wanted to move to a *pull-me* system where an individual was able to identify and get the information they needed for themselves.'

During the early life of the Intranet, usage at certain locations grew by a staggering 1,000 per cent per month. Overall growth was 100 per cent month on month.

BT's new information management policy lays down a guiding framework that devolves responsibility for the contents of the Intranet to *information owners*. Departments can set up their own Intranet home pages or sites, which provide the information they believe colleagues need. The ability to track usage of this information allows BT to measure whether it is truly valuable or not by the number of hits received.

The most popular sites attract some one million hits per month. The breadth of information available is staggering and ranges from product information, case studies and downloadable sales presentations to in-depth technical information and competitor analysis – the Intranet even contains boiler-plate contracts and quality process documentation.

Managers no longer need to act as information *filters* for their staff. They can instead concentrate more on building teams and solving problems. Employees can get the information they need to make decisions – confident that the data is accurate, timely and presented in a way which meets their needs. At £660 million in just the second year of full operation, savings are already over 10 times those forecast, with improvements in effectiveness now at 25 per cent compared to the time prior to the implementation of the Intranet. The roll-out of the Intranet shows no sign of slackening, primarily because the people driving it forward are the users themselves – people in the midst of a real information revolution.

'The reason it is so profitable,' says Charles Lowe, formerly in charge of BT's own Intranet implementation and now a consultant to customers of BT Intranet Services, 'is that it is about leveraging all the investments you made in the past, especially in people. But if you concentrate on the financials you are really missing the point. Empowered people, working in different ways, are satisfying customers better and generating much extra revenue.'

*Information provided by Julia Middleton of BT Intranet Services*

## Intranet design

The main part of the Intranet is the graphical interface which we will call the *Web* (other integral parts include: e-mail, newsgroups and discussion lists – have a look back at Sunday if you need a recap on these).

The first page of text and graphics that a user sees when they connect to the system is known as a **home page**. As such, this has to be the most important page of all the pages that you will place on your Intranet. Not only does this page have to be designed so as to attract and hold the user's attention, but it must also act as a signpost for the rest of your Intranet.

Ensure that the home-page URL (Uniform Resource Locator) is the default page seen when the user starts their browser. This way they cannot miss any important or new highlights you wish to promote.

How you group your information is dependent on your style of organisation. You may wish to keep it by function, for example, keeping all personnel information separately from marketing information, or you may wish to group by project.

The figure below shows an example of one Intranet home page.

**Figure 6**  *Sample home page*

*(Reproduced with the permission of Jakob Nielsen – Sun Microsystems, Inc)*

So that your Intranet is logical and consistent and avoids unnecessary repetition, use pieces of paper to map out its layout. Start at the home page and work downwards.

A sample Intranet design is shown overleaf.

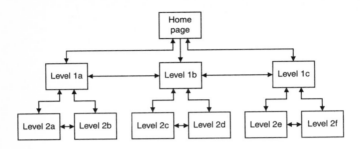

**Figure 7** *Flow chart demonstrating simple Intranet design*

Aim to keep the number of levels to a maximum of five. After this number, navigation of your Intranet becomes increasingly complex.

Initially there may be few links between the information of each function, as they probably won't know exactly what other departments are putting together. It is imperative, therefore, that the whole site be scanned through by the Intranet project team before the system goes live to add these links and avoid unnecessary duplication of information. After the Intranet has been in operation for a while, the building of links will become much easier (although they will always require checking). As your design or site-map will become the key reference point throughout the life of the site, it's important to remember to update the site-map to take any changes into account.

All of the pages on the Web will have their own URL. Users of the Intranet can tell their browser to *bookmark* the pages they visit the most (by saving the address of the page with a recognisable name), so they can jump to the page with one click of the mouse rather than having to navigate through the whole of the Intranet from top down.

Here are some top tips to remember when creating and adding pages to your Intranet:

- Never include links to pages which are 'under construction' or 'coming soon' as this frustrates users.
- Always try to view the site from the users' perspective. If you find this difficult, ask someone who has never used the Intranet before to give their opinions. Watch them while they navigate around, and identify any 'signposts' which are unclear.
- Remember to include information about where the webmaster or other members of the Intranet project team can be contacted in case of any problems. A most useful way of allowing users to contact a member of the support team is to include a *mailto* link. When this link is clicked on, a box appears allowing the user to type in a message which is then automatically sent to a designated person.

- Also include a mailto link where users can post their suggestions for improvements and additions to the Intranet. Offer some incentive for users to provide such suggestions, possibly monetary, vouchers or a gift.
- Remember that when you put information onto the Intranet, you can include links to other relevant complementary information. So, for example, a memo or press release giving details of a new product could have a link to the full product specification and price list.
- Include search engines which enable users to find information without having to navigate through a series of links. Consider placing search engines in separate sections of your site as well as on the home page. This way, searches are limited by default to (for example) the product catalogue or personnel, and the possibilities of irrelevant hits (such as information on the product 'Smith Saw' appearing alongside details about John Smith the Finance Director) are avoided.
- Remember that you can password-protect part of a site. One of the benefits of an Intranet is that it allows greater access to information for all employees, but legal or confidential stipulations may mean you need to restrict access.

## Content design

The design of a Web site is made up of two parts: the information itself and how this information looks and is displayed. Some other issues which you should consider when designing the content are:

- Place a 'button'/link on each page so that users can jump back to the main menu with one click of the mouse.
- The wording of the headings is of the utmost importance. For example, you may wish to use 'Our latest prices' rather than 'Sales information' as a heading. Ensure you have someone check out the wording before you go live: just because *you* understand the meaning does not necessarily mean someone else does. Puns can be useful, but more often than not they confuse the user.
- Remember screen resolution. Computer monitors can be configured to various resolutions. What looks reasonable at a screen resolution of 800*600 *pixels* will look a lot different at 640*480. Your identification of the hardware available in the initial stages of setting up the Intranet should give you an accurate idea of what is the most common screen resolution used in the organisation, so you can tailor the design of your content to this.
- Include the date when each page was last amended. This is an extremely effective way of helping to assure users of the information's currency.
- Don't highlight too much – only the prominent things. The overuse of graphics and flashing text (which is easy to create) is widespread on the Internet. These sites look awful and can take what seems like an eternity to download – so use it sparingly and only on those items

you particularly want to draw attention to. If you have
acknowledged that a lot of users will be dialling into
the Intranet over standard telephone lines, then test
the speed of your site by doing the same. Use a slightly
slower modem than is often used.

- Consider using icons instead of larger graphics. If users
  want to see the larger graphic, they can click on the icon,
  rather than being forced to wait for a large picture to
  download that they don't need (or want) to see.
- If the users of your Intranet are using more than one
  make of browser, you will have to test your designs on all
  of these types. This should only occur when suppliers or
  customers have access to the Intranet, as you may not
  have control over their software selection.
- *Frames* (which enable certain pieces of information
  such as site navigation aids to remain constantly on
  the screen, whilst information around them changes),
  although quite complicated to build initially, help users
  immeasurably. A good example of a frame at work is a
  margin area which displays buttons linking back to key
  items on the site (such as 'Search', 'Home', 'Press
  releases') whilst the majority of the screen displays
  the pages.

## Putting it all together – assigning responsibility

Within each of the functions that will provide content for
the Intranet, at least one person should be given the
responsibility of creating the content to the correct style
guides, placing it on the Intranet, and keeping it up-to-date.

Do not underestimate the time that this will require. Even updating the pages of a small department will probably require one to two days per month, averaged over a year.

Flat content can be fairly easily created. Word-processed documents (new or existing) can be simply converted into HTML (the standard Intranet language), and hyperlinks to other pages can then be added. The file can then be transferred across the network to its home on the Intranet server (see the diagram overleaf). Alternatively, the user can create the document in an HTML editor without having a source word-processed document.

As soon as the file is placed on the server, the content can be viewed by anyone who has access to the Intranet, but this stage must wait until the webmaster (possibly calling on the Intranet team) has checked the content and presentation of each file before it becomes live.

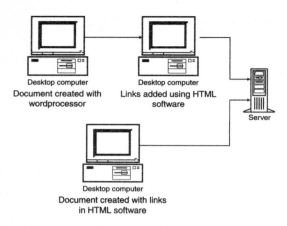

**Figure 8**   *Creating a file on the Intranet*

Even when the Intranet is successfully established, the webmaster should continue to keep responsibility for transferring files. This is because there are serious security implications should users be allowed direct access to the files on the Intranet server. This responsibility for transferring files is also essential to maintain management control of the site, so as to ensure both that guidelines are adhered to and that the site retains the feel of a whole entity rather than just a collection of vaguely linked pages – a member of the marketing department, for example, may not necessarily recognise the need for links from their pages to other departments and areas.

## Summary

Today we have looked at internal applications of an Intranet, and we've seen how easy it is to put together flat content. Tomorrow we will examine how we can involve suppliers and customers in using, and extending, our Intranet.

# External applications of Intranets

As organisations have come to value the contributions an Intranet can make to improved internal communication, reduced costs and an easing of the flow and duplication of paper, they have begun to look to expand these advantages beyond the confines of the organisation and to link with partners, customers and suppliers.

Inter-organisational computer links have been utilised for a relatively long time. Some organisations have allowed selected customers or suppliers dial-up access to their computers, and others have adopted a more formal approach known as Electronic Data Interchange or EDI. A well-known example of EDI in practice is that of supermarkets. As goods are passed through checkouts, their bar codes are used by the supermarket's computer for stock control. When stock reaches a certain level, the computer will automatically order new items from suppliers.

EDI and selected accessibility do have major drawbacks, however, most of which relate to cost. EDI is an expensive option to install. Dedicated computers often have to be purchased to ensure common standards and to allow for inter-connectability, and a communications infrastructure also needs to be put in place. EDI is also a rigid system: it is excellent at the purpose for which it was designed, but it is nearly impossible to adapt it to allow for alternative uses.

Intranets avoid many of these problems, as we have already seen. They:

- Allow communication between a variety of types of computer

- Are easy to use – simple browser technology means no complicated programming
- Are relatively cheap
- Can be adapted for virtually any use

Many organisations are now allowing their customers or suppliers access to all (or selected parts of) their Intranet. This expansion of an Intranet is becoming known as an *Extranet* – a term coined by two of the founders of Netscape Communications who used it to define software that facilitates inter-company relationships.

Today we will look at Extranets in some detail, and will examine the key considerations, namely:

- How are Extranets being used?
- What are the technical requirements of an Extranet?
- What are the security issues?
- What should we consider if we are setting up an Extranet?

## How are Extranets being used?

Here are just some of the ways in which Extranets can be put to use.

*Contact with customers*
Organisations are facing more and more demands from their customers (both individual and corporate) to be available 24 hours a day, 365 days per year. One way to achieve this is through an Extranet. Apart from continuous availability, Extranets offer huge advantages to organisations and their customers. These include:

- Improved customer satisfaction – Extranets enable better communication with customers both from and to the organisation. Customer feedback can be quickly received and problems sorted out
- Order placement and order tracking
- Basic help/problem-solving for customers to do themselves
- Proprietary technical bulletins – which by being placed on the Extranet are restricted just to customers
- Vendor–supplier interaction – fault warnings and product development can be facilitated by an Extranet
- Automated quote generation – customers can see various parts, and then quotes can be given instantaneously
- Stock checking

*Sales and marketing*

Because sales and marketing departments are often spread geographically, they gain considerable benefits from an Extranet:

- Up-to-date sales information can be distributed to reps anywhere in the world
- Orders can be taken direct from the road, rather than by posting or faxing the order request, or delivering it by hand
- Innovative sales formats can be utilised – multimedia, video-conferencing
- Up-to-date customer research can be instantly available to the sales and marketing team rather than having to wait until it is printed
- An Extranet removes the need to carry huge amounts of paperwork around and means that you never have to say you've forgotten something vital again!
- Sales support – reps can be in contact with both customers and the home-base 24 hours a day

*Product and project management*

Inter-organisational projects are facilitated through the use of an Extranet:

- Product managers can quickly create and publish the latest product or training information
- Project team members around the world can easily communicate and share results
- The location of teams is no longer important – international working is enabled

*Partnership working*

The growth in *partnership working* (between different organisations or between customers and suppliers) can be aided by the development of an Extranet:

- Input from customers (corporate or otherwise) on the design of new products can be built into a new product before it goes into production or is produced even on a trial basis
- Inter-organisational collaboration on projects can be assisted by allowing access to a restricted area of the organisation

One of the most important factors of an Extranet, but one that is often overlooked, is that it shows a commitment to customers and suppliers. By acknowledging their need for up-to-date information and access to your organisation, and then doing something about it, you will strengthen relationships with your 'partners'.

## What are the technical requirements of an Extranet?

Extranets share much technology with Intranets, and obviously with the Internet itself. As we have already seen, an Intranet requires:

> * A Web browser for each desktop or remote computer
> * A Web server
> * An appropriate protocol – although because Extranets make use of the Internet, this must at least include **Transmission Control Protocol/Internet Protocol (TCP/IP)**

Extranets additionally require:

* A device to allow connection to the outside world (either a modem or a leased line)
* Future security measures

*How can people connect to your Extranet?*
A variety of mechanisms are available to allow connection to an Extranet. These include:

* A LAN-based connection (internal staff use only)
* Remote employee access to the LAN
* Remote partner access to the Web server/Intranet – similar to a WAN
* Public Web access to the outside and into the organisation – this is often achieved through what is known as *tunnelling*. Tunnelling involves creating a secure private channel over the Internet from an external computer into an Intranet (or sometimes between two Intranets)

It is important to ascertain what computer hardware and software are being used by the customers and suppliers. Many will already have access to the Internet, but if you are expecting their usage of the Extranet to be high, then a more 'permanent' connection, possibly through a leased line, should be considered. If access to the Extranet is to be restricted to modem only, then this will impact on the applications to be offered and the design of pages.

An example Extranet may look something like the diagram below.

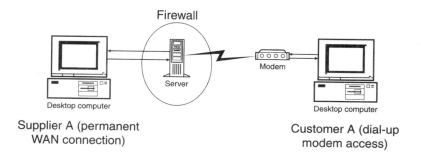

**Figure 9**  *An example of an Extranet network*

The advantages offered by an Extranet are the same for suppliers and customers as they are to your organisation, and you will need to stress these benefits when dealing with both groups. Of particular importance is round-the-clock, global access to information. Remember as well that by simplifying access to information for customers and suppliers, you should find yourself with more business than before. It may be necessary, though (if the benefits appear greater for your organisation than for your partners'), to supply equipment over which they can use the Extranet.

Generally speaking, interactive applications are more predominant when utilising Extranets than Intranets, and this brings with it a requirement for some programming skills. For example, scripts can be written in such a way that when a customer orders a product, the price is calculated automatically and an invoice is sent out. This may require you to buy-in the skills and experience to write these scripts and programs.

## What are the security issues?

We have previously seen how important security is to an Intranet. Extranets – which by definition allow for external access – need to have even more rigorous security measures. They should be able to:

- Protect resources against unauthorised access
- Encrypt communication
- Authenticate the user's ID
- Verify that the information received was the same as that sent

*Firewalls* and *encryption* are of the utmost importance here. Have a look back at the relevant section on Tuesday (see pages 42–43) if you need a refresher for these terms. It may also be necessary to consider hosting the Extranet on a stand-alone server (only the Extranet is then exposed to possible breaches of security from outside). This adds additional security, but also makes it more difficult for updated files to be transferred backwards and forwards.

## Case Study No. 3 – Mobil's Corporate Extranet

The Mobil Corporation (the international oil, gas and petrochemical company) has recently implemented an Extranet to improve order processing to its lubricant distributors. Previously, Mobil used an EDI network to distribute information, but this was expensive as a dedicated network was required and software maintenance fees were high. The open-platform systems enabled by developments in Internet technology, meant that an Internet-based solution was the most logical choice for both ease of management and cost-effectiveness.

In conjunction with Proxicom (a firm of consultants), an Extranet was developed which utilised the existing mainframe EDI systems by running Netscape SuiteSpot server software which acts as an interface between the EDI system and Web-based packages. This meant that all the processes which had been possible before could continue and some of the new developments in Internet technology could also be utilised. An example of this is the inclusion of a Java **applet** that details Mobil's business rules. This applet alerts a distributor automatically if they are entering an incorrect order, and because the applets are updated as soon as any of the business rules change, Mobil knows its distributors are using the correct set of information.

Mobil estimates that the implementation of the Extranet is saving Mobil and its distributors over $100,000 per year in systems costs associated with using a *value added network* (*VAN*) for EDI.

*Information provided by Marni Mirowitz of The Mobil Corporation*

## What should we consider if we are setting up an Extranet?

By undertaking the communication and information audit we mentioned on Monday, we should have ascertained which suppliers, customers and partners we contact on a regular basis. Ask yourself the following questions:

- Who are the organisation's suppliers and customers?
- Can this list of customers and suppliers be broken down by order of importance?
- What are the information flows from the organisation to the supplier/customer and vice versa?
- Which functions or services have been outsourced? This can range from fleet management to marketing.
- Is the organisation collaborating with a partner on a particular project?

Remember to involve the customers and suppliers in this process as well. They may be able to identify areas where they require further or improved communication and information, areas that are more difficult to determine from the inside.

The audit will also highlight the types of information that are required from customers and suppliers. This can help formulate a two-way Extranet. Not only should suppliers be able to check inventory levels, but they should also be able to supply information on the Intranet regarding their products, for example, technical manuals.

Managing an Extranet needs more commitment than an internal Intranet, as, generally speaking, all suppliers and customers will have different requirements. Its scaleable nature will help here, though, as you can begin building the Extranet with one key supplier and then expand to include others as well.

## Summary

Today we have seen that Extranets:

- Offer the same benefits of improved communication and information to external parties as Intranets do to internal employees
- Can help build stronger partnerships with key customers and suppliers
- Are not hardware- or software-dependent
- Must be made secure through the use of firewalls, passwords and encryption
- Require possibly more management commitment than Intranets because of the variety of customers and suppliers
- Can be implemented in stages, taking an initial group of suppliers or customers and then expanding to cover more

Yesterday and today, we have looked at the applications of Intranet technology. Tomorrow we shall examine the management and implementation issues this technology brings with it.

# Management and legal issues

Today we will look at some of the management and legal issues to be considered when setting up an Intranet. The key issues in the 'Implementation' stages of the Intranet project life cycle are:

- Promotion
- Data protection
- Copyright
- Libellous/illegal material
- Intranet usage policy
- Training
- Information overload
- Backups

If you are operating an Extranet as well, then the management implications must be broadened to include external partners.

## Promotion

The Intranet will have been launched in a blaze of publicity. Remember, however, that familiarity breeds contempt, and after the initial enthusiasm for the project, employees may begin to lose interest.

Continue to promote usage of the Intranet by advertising it to all employees, i.e. by writing 'press releases' to update people on new additions to its content. Although releasing these on the Intranet first will encourage non-users to become users, they need to be released on paper too so that even current non-users can see them. It is important to ensure that there are particular parts of it to which employees will want to return. Mugs, pens and mousemats displaying the Intranet logo are a good method of promotion, and you could run a competition on the best ideas for an Intranet application.

## Data protection

Many countries now have some form of legislation regulating the type of data that can be held on an individual. In the UK, the Data Protection Act (1984) is the appropriate legislation, and it has two main emphases. First, data users (normally organisations) who hold personal data on others are required to register with the Data Protection Registrar, detailing:

- The type of personal data to be held by the data user
- The purposes for which the data is used
- The source of the data
- The people to whom the data will be disclosed
- Any countries where the data may be transferred

Second, individuals are given the right to see computerised information held about themselves, and where necessary have it corrected. Information may only be collected if it meets the data-protection principles. These state that personal information shall be:

- Collected fairly and lawfully
- Only held for the lawful purposes stated
- Only used for the purposes stated in the register
- Adequate, relevant and not excessive to the purposes stated
- Accurate, up-to-date and not held for longer than required
- Accessible to the individual concerned, who has the right to have incorrect information corrected
- Kept secure

Most organisations hold some form of computerised records about their employees, so most should be registered already. If your Intranet enables access to personal information, then your organisation's registration will need to be amended.

The European Union has produced a Data Protection Directive (1995) – implemented across the EU in October 1998 – which extends the provisions of the Data Protection Act. The aim of the Directive is to protect the privacy of individuals, which obviously limits the type of information that can be collected. Organisations are not allowed to collect the following information on their employees, unless such information is statutorily required:

- Ethnic origin
- Political or religious views

- Trade union membership
- Health
- Sexuality

Further relevant information is available from the:

Data Protection Registrar
Wycliffe House
Water Lane
Wimslow SK9 5AF
Tel: 01625 535777
Fax: 01625 524510
Web: www.open.gov.uk/dpr/dprhome.htm

## Copyright

The aim of copyright is to protect an individual's or organisation's *intellectual property* from copying by others. Copyright can apply to anything created by anyone else – a poem, a report, a photograph or a portrait – and is an automatic right (unlike a patent it does not have to be applied for). Contrary to popular belief, copyright law applies to material available over the Internet – just because information is available free of charge, it does not mean it is not the copyright of someone. In the context of electronic publishing, it can apply also to e-mail messages, computer graphics or databases.

This has two key implications for the corporate Intranet. First, employees must ensure that they have permission to reproduce items subject to copyright if they wish to include these on the Intranet, and second, information held on the Intranet is the copyright property of the organisation and therefore cannot be reproduced without permission from the organisation. Not knowing the copyright law is not a defence, so ensure that all employees are aware of its implications and that they abide by these.

## Libellous/illegal material

The Internet has long had a reputation for being the home of some individuals who seem to enjoy posting inaccurate and unfair messages to, and about, others. Because of the similarity between your Intranet and the Internet itself, employees may feel that it is acceptable to post such views internally. It must be impressed on employees from the outset that the Intranet is the same as any other mechanism of corporate communication. Anything which originates from it has the same status as information sent out on company-headed note-paper, and consequently, nothing should be said or done on an Intranet which would not be said or done via more traditional forms of communication. Laws of libel and those applying to the broadcast or transmission of illegal material, apply to both the Internet and the Intranet.

This is seen very clearly from damages awarded in July 1997. The insurer Norwich Union Healthcare, had to pay over £400,000 to Western Provident (one of its competitors) after an employee of the former company posted an erroneous e-mail stating that Western Provident was insolvent. That this was posted on an internal mail system was irrelevant – Western Provident had previously obtained a court order to prevent the e-mail being deleted from the system and thus to ensure the evidence was still there.

## Intranet usage policy

These three above elements (copyright, data protection and
the law of libel) demonstrate the need to have a clearly
defined policy on what is, and is not, acceptable usage of
the company Intranet. The policy must set out clearly the
purposes for which the Intranet is designed and the
purposes to which it may be put. Disciplinary action for
failure to comply with the policy must be explained and
taken where necessary.

An example of an Intranet usage policy, containing typical
clauses, follows:

- Copyright law applies to information held on the
  Intranet. Do not place copyright items on the
  Intranet unless you have permission from the
  original author of the item. Guidance is available
  from *<name of employee responsible>*.
- Attempts to gain access to other parts of the
  organisation network through the Intranet are strictly
  prohibited, and such attempts are considered a
  disciplinary offence.
- Personal information held on the Intranet is held under
  the terms of the Data Protection Act. If you discover
  errors in information provided about you, please
  contact *<name of employee responsible>* immediately.
- Sexist, racist or libellous remarks will not be
  tolerated. Breaches of this will be treated as a
  disciplinary offence.
- Unauthorised use or attempted use of passwords will
  be treated as a disciplinary matter.

- Individuals are responsible for reporting any breach of security (including disclosure of a password) to their manager and the IT department immediately.
- Information contained on the Intranet remains company-confidential and must not be disclosed to other organisations without permission.
- Non-business use of e-mail is prohibited. To check this, Bloggs and Co. reserve the right to carry out random checks of e-mail at our discretion.
- A training session which includes this policy will be provided before Intranet access is granted. At the session, you will be required to sign a form (below) to state that you understand the policy.
- Bloggs and Co. reserve the right to increase the scope of this policy at any time.

I ............ have attended a training session for use of the Bloggs and Co. Intranet on ....... . I agree to abide by the Intranet Usage Policy and understand that failure to do so is a disciplinary offence.

Signed:                              Name:

## Training

What should be included in an Intranet training programme?

- Details of approved Internet applications
- Intranet application reference manuals
- Intranet security and access controls
- An acceptable-use policy

Don't forget that although you expect everyone to use the
Intranet, a huge range of experience in using computers
will be involved here. Some individuals will not know how
to use a mouse or what a browser is, whilst others will
have been *surfing the 'net* at home for a couple of years. It's
important therefore to set up a range of beginner,
intermediate and expert sessions that allow users to start at
a point they feel comfortable with.

Training should only be given to those who will be able to
use the Intranet now. For those departments which will gain
access later, awareness seminars detailing what is happening,
why they have not got immediate use of the Intranet and
when they can expect to have access are more useful.

*Approved Internet applications*
This section of the training programme needs to explain
both what the applications are and how they work, as well
as explaining why the full range of Internet applications is
not included (such as Internet Relay Chat). Subjects to
cover include:

- The use of bookmarks
- Using search engines to best effect
- Saving and downloading files
- Printing out from the Intranet (remembering that one of the main purposes of an Intranet is to reduce the amount of paper generated!)
- HTML (if you allow people to create their own pages)

*Reference manual*

Surely, you may say, the whole point of an Intranet is to reduce the paper mountain that exists: people can now look for help on the Intranet itself. Yes they can, but – particularly to begin with – help is required in how to access help screens. A brief *aide-mémoire* on some basics (this is what the *back button* does, etc.) will suffice, provided it is matched by some hands-on training.

*Security and access controls*

As we saw on Tuesday, your Intranet should be protected by a range of security measures including firewalls and passwords. These will only work if the people who use your Intranet understand why they are there and why they are important. Stress the need to:

- Change passwords regularly
- Not write passwords down
- Choose passwords which are at least eight characters long and which (preferably) are a mixture of numbers and letters

*Intranet usage policy*

The contents of, and the need for, an Intranet usage policy must be explained to employees during the training session.

This is also the time when they should sign the declaration stating that they understand and agree to its terms. There can then be no possibility of an employee claiming to be unaware of the existence of this policy. Stress that non-compliance with the policy will result in disciplinary action – including immediate dismissal where appropriate.

*User resistance*

Once formal training has been completed, users need to learn through experience. In order to get the return on Intranet investment which you have been expecting, employees *must* use the Intranet. Your usage log will help identify those employees who are not making extensive use of the Intranet, and you may then target them for additional training. Not everyone will understand the benefits that an Intranet can offer – sometimes they have to undergo a 'road to Damascus' type conversion before they understand – but it is important to help them try to use it.

Some organisations consider that the best way to overcome employee resistance is to announce that from a given date certain types of information (the internal telephone directory for example) will *only* be available on the Intranet. This certainly focuses the minds of employees, but it is not always the most productive way to encourage Intranet use!

## Information overload

As we have previously seen, Intranets are an excellent method to promote internal communication. However, to a certain extent they are the victims of their own success. Because they enable easy communication between employees via e-mail, information overload can be a significant problem. Part of the training programme for Intranet use should examine strategies to deal with information, ensuring that it is used to its best effect – information should be your servant, you shouldn't be its slave! Remember that the same disciplines which apply to handling paper-based information apply also to Intranets – especially those of focusing on the target audience, obeying the 'must-have' versus 'nice-to-have' information rule and, ideally, one-page management.

The following coping strategies (many of which are essential to correct Intranet usage) can help:

- Know where and how information can be obtained rather than storing it yourself in the hope that a need arises.
- Think of information in terms of useable intelligence rather than useful data: intelligence is information

with value added; data is useful figures which need thought applied to them!

- Restrict your information activities to what you need or must have: if something is interesting but fails to meet a current need, then you do not need to keep it.
- SDI. No, not the Reagan Star Wars initiative. Selective Dissemination of Information, in practice, means disciplining yourself to respect the possible information overload of other employees: only pass on e-mail or other hard-to-get information that you know will be of interest.
- Establish personal screening procedures.
- Don't forget the 'Delete' command!

## Backups

As with all other computer data held, it is essential to *backup* the Intranet. This should be done daily (at minimum), and all files amended during the course of a day should be backed up to another part of the system until they are safely secured on the formal backup.

## Summary

Today we have considered the most important management and legal issues involved in Intranets. The importance of good training for users and the establishment of an Intranet usage policy cannot be stressed too highly. Tomorrow we will review our Intranet and make recommendations for future developments.

# Evaluation and appraisal of the Intranet

Today we will look at the last stage of the project life cycle (remembering that this last stage never actually finishes!), that of evaluating your Intranet. We will also discuss ways to ensure your Intranet remains relevant and current, and finally, we provide some tips to help ensure that your Intranet is the 'killer application' it can be.

* Reviewing the Intranet's objectives
* Gathering views and opinions of the users and non-users
* Acting on the results of the review
* Keeping employees informed
* Reporting back to management
* Keeping the Intranet alive
* And finally ...

## Reviewing the Intranet's objectives

The first stage in evaluating the Intranet is to review the objectives which we set on Monday.

To recap, those example objectives we gave were to:

* Improve communication and information flow amongst employees, suppliers and customers
* Improve customer service
* Allow new ways of working, including teleworking and 'hot-desking'
* Facilitate cross-functional teams and projects

So, some of the questions we should ask ourselves include:

- Can some employees now work at home or at any terminal in the organisation?
- Do customers and suppliers have easier access to information, and has the communication flow between the organisation and these groups improved?
- Have customer response times improved?
- Has the use of cross-functional teams increased, and has their effectiveness improved?

## Gathering views and opinions of the users and non-users

The next step should be to gather the opinions of the users of the Intranet. This can be done by *posting* questionnaires on the Intranet itself.

By placing surveys regarding the usefulness of the Intranet actually on the system itself, you are, of course, only gaining the views of the users themselves. It is also important to contact non-users to find out why they are not using the Intranet, and what would make them do so. *Focus groups* are an effective method of doing this, especially as you will then be able to put questions face-to-face to non-users. Printed questionnaires can be used as well.

Questions you should ask (to internal and external users) include:

- Do you find the Intranet useful?
- If so, which parts?
- If not, why not?

- How do you think it could be improved?
- Is there anything else you think should be included on the Intranet?

You can expect to hear some surprising results through employee surveys. For example, you may have thought the Intranet was working fast enough, but the users may complain of 'congestion' and a slowing-down of the Intranet at particular times of the day. You may have to reconsider your hardware, or upgrade it. Also, be prepared to do further training and more promotion.

The usage-tracking software held on your server will provide a great deal of statistical information on which pages of your Intranet are the most regularly accessed and which are rarely looked at. Remember that if certain areas are not looked at often, this may be because they are difficult to navigate to or are 'hidden' from common viewing, not because the information they contain is not useful.

By taking a good look at usage patterns and the content of your Intranet, you will also be able to ascertain which departments are rarely contributing to the content of the system as well.

## Acting on the results of the review

Once you have completed the first review session, it is time to go back to the start of the project life cycle and make the necessary changes and modifications. This includes more than modifying the content of the Intranet itself. It also includes:

- Promoting the Intranet to specific non-user groups
- Pushing forward the new ways of working
- Looking for new users (for example, new suppliers and customers)

You could even decide to totally revamp the Intranet! This actively enforces you to start again from scratch, but this time using the experience that you have gained.

## Keeping employees informed

Let everyone know how good your Intranet is. Don't be afraid of going 'overboard' in this area. There is nothing that will catch the interest more of your employees, customers or suppliers than if they learn about how much the Intranet is used by others.

## Reporting back to management

Letting senior management know of the success of an Intranet is key. They will often only be interested in the hard business facts. You should be able to calculate the cost of savings on print material, for example, the staff handbook, quite easily. Use the results of your employee-satisfaction surveys also, as well as actual comments from users. When justifying the Intranet, focus on value gained as well as cost savings. You will be able to put together some brief examples of where work has been completed in quicker than usual time because of the benefits of the Intranet.

## Case Study No. 4 – The Intranet at Royal & SunAlliance Engineering

*From pilot to implementation*

The Intranet at Royal & SunAlliance Engineering was first piloted in response to a variety of business needs:

- To improve internal communications
- To upgrade the mainframe bulletin-board technology currently in place
- To find a more effective, flexible and secure method of distributing technical information
- To set up a more central source of information

As ours was a very paper-led and information-rich company, the initial focus was on using the Intranet as an information tool – storing and distributing information and making it more easily accessible for staff.

The company had little Internet or Intranet expertise and no available budget. The first task was to assess business needs, and representatives from all areas of the business formed a team to assess what information would be of most value to them. Their needs varied from an on-line telephone directory, to social information and personal profiles, to standards and detailed product information. We planned to pilot our pages to around

150 staff (10 per cent of employees), covering both PC and UNIX networks and all regions, to allow us to assess the impact on the network infrastructure.

The IT department was confident of its skills, but one objective of the Intranet was to rely on IT not for publishing, but only for managing the server and installing and supporting browser software. Our parent company was exploring Web technology, and with its help and a small team within Engineering, we were able to have the pilot up and running by September 1996. Subsequent development has been completed in-house, but we recognise that we may need 'professional' help with some integrated database and design work.

Throughout the autumn of 1996, the new Intranet was greeted with enthusiasm amongst the pilot group, and we managed to achieve regular updates of material and increase the extent available. Requests were constantly being received for access to the Intranet. However, the announcement of a merger between Royal Insurance and Sun Alliance Insurance in the summer of 1996 had, by late autumn, resulted in altered priorities throughout the company. It was a shame we were not six months further down the line in progressing the Intranet as it would have been a very useful tool in integrating the two companies. Throughout 1997 we have consolidated our 'Killer Applications', including a Telephone Directory, a Search Engine on the Technical Library and a Market Intelligence database. We are now awaiting budget approval for full implementation in 1998.

Lessons learned during the pilot study were:

- Staff like it
- Get people involved in contributing early on
- Adopt a flexible publishing layout
- Agree on standards and software early on
- Get senior management support early on

- Some benefits can be difficult to price
- Do not over-promise

Further applications we hope to pursue include:

- Document control and audit
- Product guide
- Remote access
- Process tracking and checking customer queries – providing the ultimate link to all the underlying databases but offering a common look and feel to the user
- Setting up discussion groups and video-conferencing
- Strengthening and building up relationships with brokers and clients by setting up links between the engineering Intranet and their own Intranets or by providing remote-access links

The pilot study has shown that the technology is suitable for us and is manageable, having little impact on other applications. Additionally, the company is keen to embrace the improvements in information sharing and communications offered by the system.

Whilst there are certain tangible cost benefits, in terms of print and distribution costs, that can be attributed to an Intranet installation, there are numerous intangible benefits also, and these combined are sufficient to justify the setting up of an Intranet – even as a mere bulletin board.

More extensive long-term benefits of the Intranet will be achieved by extending this initial bulletin-board style to an essential business tool. The Intranet will help Royal & SunAlliance Engineering respond to the fast-changing market and business needs, increasing its efficiency as an organisation and increasing the awareness and involvement of staff in the information cycle.

*Note:*
Royal & SunAlliance Engineering is the company formed from the merger of National Vulcan Engineering Insurance (owned by Sun

Alliance Insurance) and British Engine Insurance (owned by Royal Insurance) following the merger of the parent companies in July 1996.

*Information provided by Mrs Sara Wear of Royal & SunAlliance Engineering – sara.wear@eng.royalsun.com*

## Keeping the Intranet alive

There are a number of areas that the webmaster and the Intranet team will have to monitor to ensure that the system develops and maintains its full potential:

- New applications
- New users
- New and changing legislation

*New applications*
The scaleable implementation of your Intranet means that as new functions and departments are added, the need for new applications will become apparent. Groupware applications designed specifically for an Intranet are one area that is continually being developed. Although you may feel these applications are not suitable or appropriate at the moment, they require monitoring for possible future use.

*New users*
These can include new employees, partners (you may outsource a function or collaborate on a project with another organisation), suppliers and customers. The process of assessing and fulfilling their requirements will need to be undertaken again, but as your experience grows this should become easier.

*New and changing legislation*

Yesterday we made a point of noting changes in the Data Protection Act that will affect all member states of the European Union. Further changes to this legislation could come into force in the future. Actively review the area and the effects that new legislation could have on your Intranet. Appoint someone with responsibility for doing this, for example, your legal department if you have one or your personnel specialist. Remember as well that changes in legislation do not necessarily mean that applications will be restricted on your Intranet – the Intranet may even help you to comply with the changes.

## And finally ...

Here are 10 key tips that will help make your Intranet successful:

1    Get the support of senior management from the start, and ensure that everyone concerned is fully aware of this top-level commitment.

2    Plan the implementation of the Intranet using the standard tools of project management.

3    Involve people throughout all of the stages of the project. The end-users are the people who will use it everyday.

4    Make sure that the information content is exciting and relevant to all your end-users' needs. Stagnant Intranets die very quickly. One of the great advantages of Intranet technology, over and above its simplicity, is that users find it *fun.*

5    Be strong on content.

6    Look at the way work is carried out within the
     organisation. The Intranet could make it possible
     for employees to work at home, or from any place
     within or outside the organisation.

7    If considering an Extranet, include your major
     suppliers and customers in the Intranet as well.
     The competitive organisations, not only of the
     future but also of today, are those that share
     information with all of their stakeholders.

8    Rid the organisation of as much paperwork as
     possible, and make the information available on
     the Intranet instead.

9    Continue refining and improving your Intranet.
     Make this process systematic, holding regular
     review meetings of the Intranet team. Look for new
     applications, and utilise new technologies as they
     become available.

10   Communicate the success of the Intranet.
     Let management and users know about the
     improvements that are due to the Intranet.

**Applet** A small **Java** program that can be embedded into a Web page, providing functions such as calculators and simple spreadsheets. Applets differ from fully-fledged **Java** applications in that they are not allowed to access certain resources on the local computer, such as files and and serial devices (printers, scanners or **modems** etc.).

**Browser** Software primarily designed for viewing documents formatted in **Hypertext,** which form the basis of the **World Wide Web** and Intranets. It now includes the capability for sending **e-mail**, transferring files and reading newsgroups.

**Client** A software program that is used to contact, and obtain data from, a **server** software program on another computer, often across a great distance. Each client program is designed to work with one or more specific kinds of server program, and each server requires a specific kind of client. A **browser** is one such kind.

**Dial-up services** These usually refer to companies selling remote access to the Internet by use of the public switched telephone network.

**Electronic mail (e-mail)** A general term covering the electronic storage and transmission of messages across a computer network. It differs from most areas of telecommunications by its capability for 'non-real-time' use. When combined with an Internet connection, e-mail can be used to contact anybody else in the world who also has access to the Internet.

**Ethernet** The most popular method for networking computers in a **LAN**.

**Home page** This term most commonly refers to the main Web page for a business, organisation or person, or simply to the main page out of a collection of Web pages.

**HyperText Markup Language (HTML)** A means of formatting information to make it suitable for display on the **World Wide Web** or Intranet and viewable by a **browser**.

**Hypertext** This forms the basis for information held on the WWW. It is a method of providing easy access to related documents or explanatory text from within the document being viewed.

**Integrated Services Digital Network (ISDN)** This is used to refer to types of connections offered by providers of high-specification telecommunications services, in terms of both data transmission quality and speed. It can provide speeds of roughly 128,000 bits per second over normal telephone lines.

**Internet Service Provider (ISP)** A third-party organisation, usually commercial, that provides access to the Internet in some form, including **dial-up services**, usually for money.

**Java** A programming language invented by Sun Microsystems and designed for writing programs that can be downloaded through the Internet in the form of **applets**.

**Local Area Network (LAN)** A computer network limited to the immediate area. It enables high-speed communication over cables at distances of up to 5 kilometres.

**Leased line** A transmission line, leased from a telecommunications company, that is for the private use of the lessee. Leased lines usually begin and end at private premises and cannot be accessed from the public network.

**Mirror site** An exact copy of the information or files at one location. It enables greater access to the resource, and provides a backup in case of emergency.

HAVERING COLLEGE OF F & H E

107547

**Modem** A *modulator/demodulator*. This is a device for converting the digital signals produced by a computer into the analogue signals normally required by the public telecommunications networks. The fastest in common usage at the moment (V34+ modems) permit data transfer at 33,600 bits per second.

**Server** A computer, or a software package, that supplies services to the other computers on a network. Numerous software packages are available that allow a server to be a file server, **e-mail** server or **World Wide Web** server.

**Transmission Control Protocol/Internet Protocol (TCP/IP)** *Transmission Control Protocol*: a transport layer protocol which provides guaranteed delivery of packets. *Internet Protocol*: a network layer protocol which operates as the de facto standard for operating *networks* in connection with the *Internet*.

**Uniform Resource Locator (URL)** The standard way to give the address of any pages on the **World Wide Web** or an Intranet.

**Webmaster** The person responsible for the daily running of an Internet or Intranet site.

**Wide Area Network (WAN)** A network which connects sites usually at distances over 5 kilometres using the services provided by a telecommunications service provider.

**World Wide Web (WWW)** A system which cross-references, links and retrieves data from computers around the world, using what is called a **HyperText** system. A piece of software, called a **browser**, allows users to move from one page to another and from one document to another by using a mouse to click on highlighted terms or graphics. Information can be found in all forms, although text is predominant.